The Very Best of Ian McMillan

Ian McMillan is a poet, writer, performer and broadcaster. Of all those he likes performing best! He is poet-in-residence at Barnsley Football Club, Yorkshire TV's Investigative Poet and a regular on all sorts of radio stations. When not performing or watching football he enjoys sitting down. He can't drive, but then again most poets can't.

Chris Smedley lives in Brighton with his partner and three children. He has been illustrating everything from books to adverts for the past fifteen years.

Also available from Macmillan Children's Books

The Very Best of Richard Edwards
The Very Best of Vernon Scannell

Elephant Dreams
Poems by Ian McMillan, David Harmer
and Paul Cookson

Coming Soon

The Very Best of Wes Magee
The Very Best of Paul Cookson
The Very Best of David Harmer

THE VERY BEST OF...

IAN McMILLAN

A Book of Poems

Illustrated by Chris Smedley

MACMILLAN CHILDREN'S BOOKS

First published 2001
by Macmillan Children's Books
a division of Macmillan Publishers Ltd
25 Eccleston Place, London SW1W 9NF
Basingstoke and Oxford
www.macmillan.com

Associated companies throughout the world

ISBN 0 330 39365 0

Text copyright © Ian McMillan 2001
Illustrations copyright © Chris Smedley 2001

The right of Ian McMillan to be identified as the
author of this book has been asserted by him in accordance
with the Copyright, Designs and Patents Act 1988.

1 3 5 7 9 8 6 4 2

A CIP catalogue record for this book is available from the British Library.

Printed by Mackays of Chatham plc, Chatham, Kent.

Contents

Introduction

Hello! Come in, sit down, put your feet up, have a cup of tea or a glass of pop. I hope you feel as good reading this book as I felt writing it. I've been writing poems and stories for years now, since I was an infant, in fact. My first story, which I wrote for Mrs Hinchcliffe in Class 2 of Low Valley Juniors in Darfield, near Barnsley, was 'The Giant Came out of the Mousehole', and Mrs Hinchcliffe was a very wise woman, and she didn't say, 'Don't be silly, Ian, giants can't come out of mouseholes.' Instead she gave me a star and wrote 'Very imaginative' in my book. I didn't know what 'imaginative' meant, but I knew it was something to do with giants coming out of mouseholes.

Ever since, I've tried to use my imagination all the time, tried to make things up, to pretend that things are different from how they seem to be. That's why I write poems and stories, because anything can happen in a poem or a story.

Being a poet has been my job since 1981. During that time I've written hundreds, if not thousands, of poems, and I've performed them all over the place: in schools, theatres, libraries, prisons, hospitals, on the street in Mexico City and in a field near York. I'm not saying that to show off about what a busy little man I am, but because I think that these poems (and maybe all poems) should be read aloud.

Also, I want you to have a go at making some poems up. Yes, you. Everybody can write poems and lots of people can say them aloud and when you've finished reading this book (or maybe halfway through, or maybe even halfway through the first poem), have a go at writing some poems and then saying them aloud.

Enjoy the book! Enjoy the cup of tea or the glass of pop!

Ian McMillan

Stale

You know how sometimes
you open your sandwich box
and it smells stale

and there are a few crumbs
and a biscuit wrapper
and a bit of a crisp

and you want to close it
although you know you should wash it
you want to close it.

Well, that's how I feel today.

Counting the Stars

It's late at night
and John is counting the stars.

He's walking through the woods
and counting the stars.

The night is clear
and the stars are like salt

on a black tablecloth.
John counts silently,

his lips moving, his head tilted.
It's late at night

and John is counting the stars
until he walks into a tree

that he never saw
because he was counting the stars.

Look at John
lying in the woods.

The woodland creatures are gathering around him
laughing

in little woodland voices.

Moral:
Even when you're looking up,
Don't forget to look down.

School in the Holidays

Down the corridors
nothing happens.

In the window's light
nobody moves.

The race is over,
the engine is cooling

and the school is like a driver
removing his gloves.

New Day

The day is so new
you can hear it yawning,
listen:

The new day
is yawning
and stretching

and waiting to start.

In the clear blue sky
I hear the new day's heart.

Unexplained Things
about My Dad

Inside his favourite hat
there's strange piano music:
Listen.

At the back of his head
there's a tattoo of a polar bear riding a bike:
Look.

If you get very close to his thumb
there's the scent of a tropical storm:
Smell.

Run your hands over his left ear
and you can feel the outline of a tree:
Touch.

If he gives you a mint
it has the same flavour as pencil shavings:
Taste.

Ready Salted

Nothing else happened
that day.

Nothing much, anyway.

I got up, went to school,
did the usual stuff.

Came home, watched telly,
did the usual stuff.

Nothing else happened
that day,

nothing much, anyway,

but the eyeball in the crisps
was enough.

Ten Things Found in a Shipwrecked Sailor's Pocket

A litre of sea.
An unhappy jellyfish.
A small piece of a lifeboat.
A pencil wrapped around with seaweed.
A soaking feather.
The first page of a book called *Swimming is Easy*.
A folded chart showing dangerous rocks.
A photograph of a little girl in a red dress.
A gold coin.
A letter from a mermaid.

Ten Things Found in a Wizard's Pocket

A dark night.
Some words that nobody could ever spell.
A glass of water full to the top.
A large elephant.
A vest made from spiders' webs.
A handkerchief the size of a car park.
A bill from the wand shop.
A bucket full of stars and planets, to mix with the dark
  night.
A bag of magic mints you can suck for ever.
A snoring rabbit.

Legs of My Uncles

Uncle John's are short,
Uncle Stan's are hairy,
Uncle Jim's are long,
Uncle Frank's are scary.

(By Ian McMillan and Andrew McMillan)

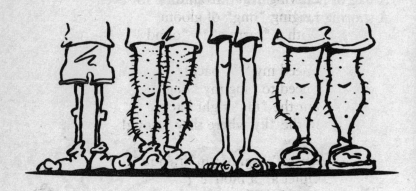

Beware of the Gho*t

There'* a gho*t in my hou*e
Quiet a* a mou*e
teal the letter '*'
Leave* my life a me**

Take* the letter*
From the *ugar and the *oap
Replace* them with *tar*
I don't think I can cope!

There'* a gho*t in my room
Leaving *tar* around
*inging *ong* of gloom
With a *tarry e**y *ound

I need my '*'* back!
I need to *ing my *ong*!
Put the *tar* right back
In the *ky where they belong!

There'* a gho*t in my hou*e
Quiet a* a mou*e
teal the letter '*'
Leave* my life a me**.

On the Tenth of February

My brother brought the snowman in
to keep him warm.

He sat him in the chair
by the fire.

The chair that Dad likes.

The snowman sat there,
sweating.
His nose began to slip away.

My dad came in from work,
freezing.

The snowman was wearing
Uncle Frank's old hat.

My dad doesn't like Uncle Frank.

My dad's glasses steamed up
in the warm room.

'Hello, Frank,'
he said to the snowman,

'When are you going to give me
that ten quid you owe me?'

The snowman collapsed
in a puddle all over the carpet.

My dad stared
at the empty chair
and said,

'It's OK, Frank,
pay me whenever you like.
It's only money.'

Out of Season

It's October, and the sun
won't hang about too long
in this broken neck of the woods.

The coaches have stopped arriving.
July, August have sizzled briefly
like chips thrown into the pan

    and in the breeze
    the trees
    are hands
    shaking with age.

All over the country
in grey village squares like this
under sky
the colour of an old man's cardigan
the year shuffles into winter,

and the village's six children
if they lived near the sea
would walk by the sea.

Instead they walk
from the phone box
to the bus stop

and from the phone box
to the fish and chip caravan.

This is a postcard
no one sends home. Nobody
wishes they were here.

From the phone box
you can see the bus stop
and little else

and in the breeze
the trees
are hands
shaking with age.

This Little Poem

This little poem has five lines
and five words in every line.
I wrote it out five times
between five o'clock and five past nine
using five different pencils every time
and this little poem tells lies.

Scottish Summer Haiku

Sun oan ma bald heid
reflecting like a mirror
blinding thae tourists!

Captain Fat and Tired's Haikus

1

Red trunks worn outside
like the great bright shining sun
in grey costume sky.

2

Behind the tight mask
he is a man with red marks
from the too-tight mask.

3

Sleep safely at night,
the hero is wide awake
until he nods off.

4

It's morning again;
what crimes has he slept through?
Who cares? Fry-up time!

Hiker

Walked five miles today
and seven miles yesterday.
Five more tomorrow.

Hiker 2

Walked seventeen miles
then had a long rest on this
old Japanese form.

Three Lineups

*Note: A lineup is an English form of poetry,
always about football, in 4-4-2 or 3-5-2
syllables, invented by me.*

1

What an own goal!
Now don't point at
Keeper!

2

Going early,
Miss the last goal . . .
Or two!

3

Penalty!
Now, please don't miss it!
Oh, no!

Three Wilsons

*Note: A Wilson is a form invented by Herbert Wilson
(1817–1888) where the poem has five lines and each
line must rhyme apart from the third line which must
contain a non-rhyming reference to a vegetable.
Sounds complex: it ain't!
(Actually, I made all that up.)*

1 Sunrise Wilson

Such a dazzling sunrise,
A delight for the eyes,
Like a big glowing turnip
A sunrise seems wise:
The dawn's daily prize!

2 Storm Wilson

Waves fall with a crash
And a great noisy splash
The spray looks like peas
In the bright lightning flash
As the thunder's teeth gnash!

3 Snow Wilson

Snow like a white hat
On the high-rise flat
White as mashed potato
Or a white welcome mat
Or Mrs Smith's cat.

An Interesting Fact about One of My Relatives

My

great great great great
great great great great
great great great great
great great great great
great great great great
great great great great
great great great great

grandad is very old.

Can't Be Bothered
to Think of a Title

When they make slouching in the chair
an Olympic sport
I'll be there.

When they give out a cup
for refusing to get up
I'll win it every year.

When they hand out the gold
for sitting by the fire
I'll leave the others in the cold,

and when I'm asked to sign my name
in the Apathetic Hall of Fame
I won't go.

Wherezebeen and Lazyboy

When the crime has been committed
and the police have been and gone
Wherezebeen and Lazyboy
get their costumes on.

When the police have done their duty
and the crime is all wrapped up
Wherezebeen and Lazyboy
make some tea and drink a cup.

When the criminal is captured
and the police go home at ten past five
Wherezebeen and Lazyboy
finally arrive.

'Where's the police gone, Lazyboy?'
'Wherezebeen, where is the crime?'
Wherezebeen and Lazyboy
wander homewards, take their time.

Going to Sleep

Going to sleep is a funny thing,
I lie in bed and I'm yawning
and Dad is reading a story and then . . .

suddenly it's morning!

First Appearance
of a Superhero in a Book

(From 'A Child's Lovely Box of Happy Verses', 1598)

Af the peafantf cowered in their hovelf
and a madman ftole their pigf
a handfome fquire climbed off hif horfe
in bright red hofe and golden wig.

'I am Fuper Fquire Dogoodneff!'
he faid, and then he fang hif fong:
and he fang all fifty verfef
and the fong waf rather long.

And af he fang, the madman
ran off with hif booty
af the peafantf liftened to the fong,
it waf their ferfly duty.

When the fong waf ended
the Fquire faid, 'Thatf my fong
now let'f catch the villain!'
But 'twaf too late for he had gone.

Fo Fuper Fquire Dogoodneff
climbed on hif fteed.
'He if ufeleff, Fquire Dogoodneff,'
the peafantf all agreed!

New Season Poem

Here comes the season
like a rider on a hoss
and I've got reason
to cheer because

Here comes the season
like a pilot in a plane
and the glory days'll
be here again!

Here comes the season
like a comet in the sky
and the New Stand's gleaming
and the hopes are high.

Here comes the season,
enjoy it while it's here
cos I feel that this
is gonna be our year!

*(Remind me of this if our season turns out to be
not all that good!)*

The Thorax: Super Ant

Super Ant, that's me.
The Thorax.
Down here,
on the floor,

like a full stop in a cape.

That's me, Super Ant.
The Thorax.
Creeping slowly
under the door,

like a comma in a mask.

Villains never see me.
Actually, that's a disadvantage.
My small voice
shouting,
'Now you're in trouble . . .'

like somebody whispering fifteen streets away.

Super Ant, that's me.
The Thorax.
Crushed
by a boot,

like an exclamation mark in tights.

It hurts.

Goldilox Girl

Through the three bears' cottage,
in a whirl,
yellow hair flowing:
Goldilox Girl!

Eat up the porridge,
do a twirl,
break the chair,
Goldilox Girl!

Through the woods,
doing good,
helping Little Red Riding Hood!

No time to settle,
feel her mettle,
cutting through the cage to Hansel and Gretel!

She's a diamond,
she's a pearl,
fairy tale heroine:
Goldilox Girl!

Elephant Dreams

1

I'm so small
I can crawl
under a leaf

and I can look
into the world
from underneath.

2

There's a huge grey cloud in the sky.
It's me
I float down onto a sycamore
tree.
I burst like a bag and the rain falls
out.
I swim in my rain like a big grey
trout.

3

My
long
trunk
goes
round
the
world
twice!

4

I am the last elephant
and I stare into the sun
as it falls into the night
and in the fading light
I know my race is run.
I am the last elephant.

5

I can't move.
People are staring at me.

I can't move.
People are walking by.

I can't move.
Children are pointing at me.

I can't move.
Is this where you go when you die?

Spot the Hidden Part of a Loaf

Look carefully
because within this poem
is hiddenCRUST
the name of a part
of a loaf.

ThisCRUST
part of a loaf
is just in the poem
for a laugh.

SomebodyCRUST said
to me,
'I bet you can't hide
part of a loaf
in a poem.'

CRUST

Have you spotted it yet?
Have you spotted it yet?

Batman's Exercise Video

Pull on the tights
Yeah, pull on the tights
Pull up the trunks
Yeah, pull up the trunks

I said twirl the cape
        twirl the cape
        twirl the cape
        twirl the cape

Pull on the boots
Yeah, pull on the boots
Snap on the mask
Yeah, snap on the mask

I said twirl the cape
        twirl the cape
        twirl the cape
        twirl the cape

Repeat until opponents are fully dazzled . . .

Coming Out of the Cinema in the Afternoon

I think
I'm still
in the film
and I'm blinking;

I blink,
I'm a still
from the film
and I'm thinking

'Keep still
don't blink
keep thinking
and the film

will still
keep blinking
as I'm thinking
I'm the film.'

Alphabet Weather

Wind

Walking wearing wellingtons
William's waving wildly:
Where's Walter?
Where's Winnie?
Whooshed Westward!
Whirled windward!

Snow

Slipping, sliding, slopping,
Susan's sucking slush.
Sue, stop!
Stop slurping!
Slush sandwich
signals stomachache!

Fog

Fat fog fingers
fondle Fiona's face.
Feel fog fish fumble
frighten Fiona,
fearful Fiona,
freezing foggy flames . . .

Goodnight, Stephen

At first it was the smell,
the smell of a torch
drifting up like mist through the field.

Then it was the sound,
the sound of a torch,
a noise like a torchbeam unzipping the tent.

Now it's the weight,
the weight of a torchbeam
across the sleeping-bag onto my face.

I must be asleep
but I think I'm waking up.

The stink of the torchbeam
smells awful, smells scary.
A torchbeam feels spiky.

The taste of the torchbeam
tastes rotten, tastes fishy.
A torchbeam feels chilly.

I think I'm waking up.
I can't be asleep.

Then it was the smell,
the smell of a pipe
through the flap of the tent,

and it was the sound,
the sound of my dad
saying, 'Just checking. Good night.'

Now it's the weight, the weight of my head
on the pillow as darkness returns.

Cautionary Playground Rhyme

Natasha Green
Natasha Green
Stuck her head in a washing machine

Washing Machine
Washing Machine
Round and round Natasha Green

Natasha Green
Natasha Green
Cleanest girl I've ever seen

Ever seen
Ever seen
A girl with her head in a washing machine?

Washing machine
Washing machine
Last home of Natasha Green

Natasha Green
Natasha Green
Washed away in a white machine

White machine
White machine
Soaped to death Natasha Green

Natasha Green
Natasha Green
Cleanest ghost I've ever seen!

Moral:
Washing machines are for knickers and blouses
Washing machines are for jumpers and trousers
Keep your head out of the washing machine
or you'll end up as spotless as little Miss Green!

Cautionary Tale for Rhyming Poets

Ian McMillan
was a poet
whose poems
occasionally rhymed.
Sometimes they did
and sometimes they didn't
and nobody seemed to
care.

Sometimes his poems
were free as sweet papers
blowing in the breeze

and they were sometimes as noisy
as wallpaper scrapers
scratching the leaves
off the autumn trees . . .

But Ian McMillan
was a poet
whose poems
occasionally rhymed.
Sometimes they did
and sometimes they didn't
and nobody seemed to
bother.

And then he got bitten
by the Rhyming Bat
that flies through the forest at night
and rhyme began
to seep into his poems
before the morning light . . .

Because the Rhyming Bat
is a deadly bat
whose bite leaves you desperate for rhyme
and you rhyme all the time
and you rhyme and you rhyme
and your poems go on rhyming all day
and the rhymes won't stop coming
like some incessant drumming
and the rhyming is rhyming to stay.

Ian McMillan
was a poet
whose poems occasionally rhymed.
Sometimes they did
and sometimes they didn't
and nobody seemed to mind,

nobody seemed to mind,

nobody seemed to mind.

Moral:
Try not to get bitten
by the Rhyming Bat
or that will be
the end of that.

Cautionary Mystery

That feller
in the yeller cap
who sits with a blanket
on his lap,

what happened to him,
what happened?

That poor old man
in the yeller hat
with a face like a cat
that's missed its flap,

what happened to him, Mum?
What happened to him?

You don't want to know, kid.
You don't want to know.
It's so terrible
you don't want to know.

But that man just sits there
on his own
with a face like a sock
and a heart like a stone.

You don't want to know, son,
you just don't want to know.

But that man just sits there,
deep in thought,
with a face like a battle
that's just been fought
and hands that shake
like leaves in a breeze
and a face like rubble
and eyes like cheese.

You don't want to know, son,
you don't want to know.

Moral:
Some things are better left unsaid
with eyes like butter and a face like bread.

Little Billy Jones and
His Nasty Mother

Little Billy Jones
had a box of rhino bones,

he kept them hidden
underneath his bed.

Mrs Lily Jones
hated Billy's rhino bones

so she chucked them in the river
and she said,

> 'I'm sorry, Billy,
> been so silly,
> you'll never guess what I've done!
>
> I've committed a sin,
> put your bones in the bin,
> now they're on the tip, my son!'

Little Billy Jones
loved his box of rhino bones,

he wept and wailed
and wailed and blubbed and wept.

Mrs Lily Jones
forgot Billy's rhino bones

and the story would have ended there
except . . .

> Listen to the pounding of the rhino feet
> up the Jones's suburban street,
> listen to the sound of the rhino roar
> up the Jones's path, at the Jones's front door.

See Lily Jones
quite forlorn
impaled on a great sharp
rhino horn.

See Lily Jones
somehow aloof
squashed beneath a two-ton
rhino hoof.

Lily Jones was Billy's mother.
Now she's flatter than a knife.
She didn't know that when you add water to rhino bones
it brings the rhino to life,

ho ho,

it brings the rhino to life!

Moral:
If you chuck bones in the river
make sure they're your own.

Coded Nursery Rhymes

*Note: The code increases in difficulty, but here's a clue:
it's a bit fishy. See if you can crack it. Good luck!*

1 An Easy One

Jack and Jill went up the fish
to fetch a pail of water.
Jack fell down and broke his fish
and Fish came tumbling after.

2 A Harder One

Little Fish Horner
sat fish a fish
eating a Christmas fish.
He fish in his fish
and fish fish fish plum
and said,
'Fish Fish Fish Fish Fish I.'

3 A Very Hard One

Fish Fish
fish fish fish wall.
Fish Fish
fish fish great fish.
Fish fish fish fish
and fish fish fish fish
fish fish fish fish again.

The Fog and Me

It was so foggy today
I couldn't see my hand
in front of my face.

I know because I waved at myself
and I didn't wave back.

Mrs White on Christmas Day

Mrs White, Mrs White,
Mouth turned down
Headscarf tight.

Every Christmas day, Mrs White,
Our next door neighbour,
Would come to watch the Queen's speech
On the television.
My dad was terrified of her,
Even though he's fought in the war
Seen ships sink and men die.

Mrs White, Mrs White,
Sitting beneath
The fairy lights.

At about ten to three
Mrs White would come in.
My mother fussed around her
With shortbread and sherry.
My dad would disappear to the kitchen
And think about Christmas at sea,
The boat heaving up and down
On waves as dangerous as Mrs White.

Mrs White, Mrs White
Once tore the tail
Off my best kite.

One Christmas Mrs White said she was cold.
My dad went to get some coal to put on the fire,
He ran into the room, slipped, ripped
The handle off the bucket, and all the coal
Went all over Mrs White. The Queen laughed.
My dad didn't.

Mrs White, Mrs White,
Sitting there
As black as night.

No Bread

I wish I'd made a list,
I forgot to get the bread.
If I forget it again
I'll be dead.

We had blank and butter pudding,
beans on zip.
Boiled eggs with deserters,
no chip butty: just chip.

I wish I'd made a list,
I forgot to get the bread.
My mam got the empty bread bin
and wrapped it round my head.

Our jam sarnies were just jam
floating on the air.
We spread butter on the table
cos the bread wasn't there.

My mam says if I run away
she knows I won't be missed,
not like the bread was . . .
I wish I'd made a list!

Self-Portrait

Face a red planet
smudged by glasses, he's
slumped in the bus seat

as the sun rises, illuminating
the little bits of whisker
he's missed, iron filings

on the nodding red planet.
How small his hands are.
How Elvis his hair is.

He may be a collapsing balloon,
chins folded like dough,
sun reflects on the glasses.

Homework

I love my school so very much
that I'm taking it home
bit by bit in my bag.

My mother says it's stealing
but I don't think it's stealing,
it's really just collecting.

I've got three bricks
and a desk so far.

The bricks were easy
but the desk was hard.

Fred

I'm Fred, the school caretaker
without a head,
look at me
I'm Fred, the school caretaker
without a head.

My head fell off in bed the other night,
I looked at my wife and she died of fright,

I'm Fred, the school caretaker
without a head.

When I go to the pub me mates say flippin 'eck
cos I carry the beer on top of me neck.

I'm Fred, the school caretaker
without a head.

Some vandals came to school and they seemed pretty
   rough
but I just had to look at them, that was enough.

I'm Fred, the school caretaker
without a head.

Needle Song

I'm knee-deep in needles
come paddle with me
as I splash in the needles
from my Christmas tree!

I'm waist-deep in needles
come travel with me
through the mountains of needles
from my Christmas tree!

Needles drop off
one by one
like a dripping
needle tap
then the needle drizzle
starts
like applause begins
with a single clap;
then the needle storm explodes
and needles rain
across the room
landing, piling, drifting high
like a spiky green needle
typhoon . . .

I'm face-deep in needles
please come and help me,
I'm eaten by needles
from my Christmas tree!

Yes, I'm eaten by needles
from my Christmas tree!

The Dog Who Knew Too Much

Fido was a brainy hound,
knew how many pennies in a pound;

by tapping his paw on the kitchen floor
could tell you who won the First World War.

His owner (not a clever bloke)
put him up for a quiz show for a joke.

Then a letter came from the TV
'Mr Fido,' it said, 'Report at 3,

make yourself known at Studio 4;
someone will take you to the studio floor.'

Fido's owner had a cunning plan:
'I'll dress my dog up like a man,

I'll hide behind his chair and shout
when he taps the answers out!

I'll win the prize then home I'll go
and nobody will ever know!'

Well, on the door, it seemed all right;
Fido was bushy-tailed and bright,

tapping all his answers out,
the audience began to whoop and shout,

until Fido won a million quid
then try and guess what Fido did.

He pushed his owner to one side
then zoomed off on a global ride

by boat and train and limousine
and from that day to this he's not been seen.

And the moral of this fable is:
never let a dog do a TV quiz,

always answer for yourself
or your hound will leave you on the stupid shelf.

Yes, your hound will leave you on the stupid shelf.

New Poem

This poem
is so new
it's not
written yet.

No lines
to remember,
no words
to forget.

This poem
is so new
it's still
in my brain.

It's waiting
to start
like a bus
or a train.

This poem
is so new
you could
write it yourself,

then write
twenty more
to put
on your shelf!

Another Christmas Present
from Auntie Mabel

What a silly present.
I can't understand it.

I don't eat seaweed because it tastes foul.
I don't wear seaweed because it looks awful.
I don't take seaweed for walks because it slips off the lead.
I don't watch videos on seaweed because they get smelly.
I don't play football with seaweed because it doesn't
   bounce.

I can't understand it.
What a silly present.

Breakfast

It cracked open the shell,
It gave off an awful smell!

It came from within my egg,
It was a horrible leg!

It seeped out of the yolk,
I thought it was a joke!

It burst out of the white
And gave me a terrible fright!

It jumped up on my shoulders,
So I hit it with my soldiers!

It fell into my spoon,
So I flicked it round the room!

It landed on my plate,
And
    Then
       I
        Saw
          Its
            MATE!

(By Ian McMillan and Andrew McMillan)

My New Shoes

All that running!
All that climbing!
All that walking!
All that kicking!
All that skipping!
All that dancing!

Just waiting
    waiting
in this box

for me to put them
over
    my
       socks!

The Dragon's Birthday Party

It's the dragon's birthday party,
he's ten years old today.
'Come and do your special trick,'
I heard his mother say.

We crowded round the table,
we pushed and shoved to see
as someone brought the cake mix in
and the dragon laughed with glee.

It was just a bowl with flour in
and eggs and milk and that
with ten blue candles round the top
in the shape of Postman Pat.

The dragon took a big deep breath
stood up to his full size
and blew a blast of smoke and flame
that made us shut our eyes.

We felt the air grow hotter
we knew the taste of fear.
I felt a spark fly through the air
and land on my left ear.

But when we looked,
make no mistake:
the candles were lit
and the cake was baked.

Marching Song of the Doorknob People

All our doors have doorknobs
All our doors have doorknobs
All our doors have doorknobs
And we march along!

A door without a doorknob
Is just a plank of wood;
Doors all need their doorknobs
Are we understood?

Hinges, letterboxes
Are important to a door
But a door without a doorknob's
Like a room without a floor!

All our doors have doorknobs
All our doors have doorknobs
All our doors have doorknobs
And we march along!

Names of Scottish Islands to Be Shouted in a Bus Queue When You're Feeling Bored

Yell!
Muck!
Eigg!
Rhum!
Unst!
Hoy!
Foula!
Coll!
Canna!
Barra!
Gigha!
Jura!
Pabay!
Raasay!
Skye!

Christmas Eve Storm at Sea

to Be Shouted in a Bus Queue

Great waves like snowdrifts
and the wind shouting a lost reindeer call;

lifeboat like a Christmas toy
up and down in the sea's lift,

lifeboat captain, fresh from a party
paper hat plastered down on his head,

lifeboat crewman, straight from his grotto
beard waving like seaweed.

The wind shouting a lost reindeer call
and the great waves like snowdrifts.

Routes

1 The Walk to School

Down Barking-dog Lane
past the street with the boat
   Clouds rush by
   Sometimes it rains

Up Old-lady-waving Road
past the field with the car
   Clouds hang still
   Aeroplanes drone

Down Skateboard Steps
past the shop with the cat
   Clouds make shapes
   Reflect in windowpanes

2 The Drive to School

radio shouts
Mum shouts
belt tight
window steam
Dad shouts
radio shouts
feel hot
feel sick
radio, Mum,
Dad shout
shout shout
every day
same shout
same hot
same sick
same same
same same

69

The Boxing Day Ghost

I am the ghost
of Boxing Day.

I live in broken presents
chucked away.

I live in all the turkey
not yet eaten;

in the crying children
my heart's beating.

I am the ghost
of Boxing Day

in the room full of relatives
with nothing to say

as Granny falls asleep
and Uncle spills his beer

my laugh is the thin, cold
sound you hear

and I'll be back
in another year:

the slob who lurks behind
the Christmas cheer.

Smashed Glasses

Through glasses smashed the world
like this looks.
Can't you see you are where or
your read books.
Cracks everything's full of and
different in a place.
Should glasses your have in glasses your
kept case.

My Grandad's Hat

He really is,
he's hat.

Years ago
he was red braces
and football boots
and brightly coloured shirts,

but now
he's hat.

Flat
hat.

Mrs Jones

Cars and lorries
come to a stop
at Mrs Jones's
lollipop!

Cars and lorries
slow right down,
her lollipop's
the best in town!

Better than
a traffic cop
is Mrs Jones's
lollipop!

Time Slips Backwards
in My Auntie's House

When we sat down to tea
it was twenty past three.

When the cakes had all gone
it was quarter to one.

When I got up to go
I was caught in the flow;

I felt myself yawn,
day had melted to dawn,

Time had sprung a big leak!
I'd slipped into last week!

Walking Through the Year

Spring walk
Warm walk

Summer walk
Hot walk

Autumn walk
Cool walk

Winter walk
Cold walk.

Strange Books on a High Shelf

My Journey to the Centre of the Sun   222 pages,
some smoking.

The New No-eat Diet   333 pages,
some chewed.

The Great Treacle Flood of 1836   444 pages,
some sticky.

How to Turn a Book into a Clock   444 pages,
some ticky.

Cooking with Paper and Ink   333 pages,
some stewed.

The Book of Exaggerations   2,222,222 pages,
I'm joking!

No Points

September, and my team
has got no points;
played six, lost six.

Our season
has creaking joints;
played six, won none.

September, and my team
are rolling down a hill
called Played Six, Lost Six.

Our season
is feeling ill
with Played Six, Won None.

Our Neighbour Never Gives the Ball Back

Best ball
over the wall!

Second best ball
over the wall!

Third best ball
over the wall!

Yellow toy ball
over the wall!

Tennis ball
over the wall!

Balloon
over the wall!

Sister's doll's head
over the wall!

Orange
over the wall!

Blown up paper bag
over the wall!

Football boot
over the wall!

Other football boot
over the wall!

Mirror Kissing

I practise kissing
in the mirror.

I close my eyes and kiss
the cool, cool glass,

open my eyes
and see my face too close,

close my eyes,
open my mouth,

kiss the mirror,
move my lips about.

The mirror goes misty,
I can't see my face;

just a steamy, sticky
kissing place.

A Very Silly Moment at the Station Platform Told in Three Different Ways

Train came in
man next to me
ate his umbrella
rain came in
and next to me
a rat and a fella
trained to sing
managed to be
quivering jelly.

I was waiting for the 9.25 when I saw the following:
An outbreak of umbrella chewing
A sound of a rat and a man singing
The sight of the man and the rat wobbling.

This kid was staring
just because I was eating my umbrella,
singing with a rat,
and bobbing about!

Moon Trousers Trousers Moon

This is just a daft idea. Get two words and stick other words near them to make new meanings. Try it yourself with other words, like Carrot and Peg, for instance. Carrotfire over the mountains. Pegfire in a domestic setting.

Fetch me the Moontrousers.
It's a Trouser Moon.
Moonsalt, if you have it.
I'm afraid I've got Trousersalt.

Moonfire over the mountains
Trouserfire in a domestic setting.
The moongull.
The trousergull.

The Moonbook. The Trouserbook.
Beware of the Moonzebra.
Beware of the Trouserzebra.
The Trouser Song. Moon Song.

I speak the old Moon Language.
I speak the old Trouser Language.
Hello, Captain Moon.
Hello, Captain Trouser.

Moongrammar.
Trousergrammar.
Moonpuzzle.
Trouserpuzzle.

Help, I have lost my Moonbiscuit!
Hoorah, I have found my Trouserbiscuit!
Hoorah, I have lost my Moonpain!
Help, I have found my Trouserpain!

Moon Electricity.
Trouser Electricity.
Moonpower.
Trouserpower.

Moon Trouser.
Trouser Moon.
Trouser like the Moon.
Moon like a trouser.

Moon.
Trouser.
Trouser.
Moon.

Index of First Lines

Index of First Lines

The very best poetry available from Macmillan

The prices shown below are correct at the time of going to press. However, Macmillan Publishers reserve the right to show new retail prices on covers which may differ from those previously advertised.

The Very Best of Richard Edwards   0 330 39389 8
£3.99

The Very Best of Ian McMillan   0 330 39365 0
£3.99

The Very Best of Vernon Scannell   0 330 48344 7
£3.99

All Macmillan titles can be ordered at your local bookshop
or are available by post from:

Book Service by Post
PO Box 29, Douglas, Isle of Man IM99 1BQ

Credit cards accepted. For details:
Telephone: 01624 675137
fax: 01624 670923
E-mail; bookshop@enterprise.net

Free postage and packing in the UK
Overseas customers; add £1 per book (paperback)
and £3 per book (hardcover)